OWN
Your
POWER

Your Guide to Feeling
Powerful, Fearless & Free

BAILEY FRUMEN, MSW, LCSW

Foreword by Fabienne Fredrickson

ISBN-13: 978-0-692-80007-2

Cover Design: Eric Angello, Quiver Creative, QuiverCreative.com

Editors: Bryna Haynes & Rebecca van Laer, TheHeartofWriting.com

Printed in the United States.

DEDICATION

This book is dedicated to my daughter, Phoebe:
may she always own her power.

ADVANCE *Praise*

"Bailey is an incredible leader and the perfect guide to take you from stressed and stuck to on-purpose and flourishing in all areas of your life. *Own Your Power* will give you the exact tools you need to effortlessly create the life of your dreams. She's the real deal."

- **LULA BROWN,** Integrative Nutrition Health Coach & Founder of
Good Taste By Lula

"This book makes it clear that as ambitious women, we are not alone. Our tribe is out there, a life by design is possible, and there is a path forward. Bailey is a heart-centered, authentic representation of the journey we all want to be on. Her personal story and success are a testament to the fact that she has done the work and has created a process that we can all follow to cash in on our own golden ticket of life. This book is a must read for anyone who wants to be the architect of their own experience and all the joy that is possible with it."

- **JENNIFER FLYNN,** The Balance Maven & Host of
Life Coach Radio Networks

"I love that Bailey shares her story of feeling overwhelmed. As I read I felt like I could relate to every line. I also really like the emphasis she puts on clarity. I think this is so hard for most people because they think they'll be able to see beyond the fog without taking any action. Bailey makes it clear that action comes first and then the fog clears. I cannot wait to read more!"

— **CHRISTINE ZILINSKI**, Concrete Education & Salon Concrete

"Bailey's story really resonated with me because it sounded so much like my own. Being an overachiever my entire life inevitably caused me to burn out! I, too, didn't know how to slow down or what that meant or looked like. I think so many women go through this without finding the answer of what that looks like for them. I love that this book provides the tools that women need to navigate their own personal journey while feeling understood and heard in their struggles. Thank you, Bailey for being brave enough to take the leap into the unknown so that you could share your beautiful gifts with the world."

— **GENA SHINGLE JAFFE**, Attorney for Entrepreneurs

"Forget trying to find balance, and focus on what you can actually control -- your own well-being! Frumen's friendly, informative writing style makes for a fluid read—easy to curl up with at the end of a long working day. I know that this will be a go-to resource that I'll pick up again and again."

— **JEN LEVITZ**, Marketing Architect

"After reading *Own Your Power,* my biggest a-ha was realizing that being an achiever can be empty and that unless we connect to ourselves and write our own rules, life will feel like an empty shell. Bailey's book has inspired me to begin challenging more of what I'm choosing in my life, be more aware, and release the need to always be 'doing.' This book is a must-read for every powerful and accomplished woman. If life feels empty or meaningless, this is your compass back to a life of passion, purpose and fulfillment."

— **KATIE MAZZOCCO**, Founder of FullSpectrumProductivity.com

"We create our life plan early on and execute it with passion and dedication—until we realize it isn't what we thought it was supposed to be. If this describes you, then this is the book for you. In *Own Your Power*, you can shift from what you're doing (being overcommitted, looking for perfection) to looking at why you live your life and your inner desires, which requires skills of introspection and space to let new answers arise. Bailey provides you with actionable tools and skillful, practical guidance to recast your life and reclaim your power so you can fully engage in life, not just survive the day."

- **MARIJO PULEO**, Host of Mindful Living Spiritual Awakening

"Wow! If only I had read this book five years ago, it would have saved me so much time, stress, and money! As an ambitious, high-achieving woman, this book speaks to my soul. Bailey reveals that you really do have the power to change your own life. If you're over-stressed and ready to take control, this book is for you!"

- **CRYSTAL CAVE**, Celebrity Wardrobe Stylist & Founder of Style Icon Academy

"Finally, a book about power that is written *for* women; strong, smart, and ambitious, yet not driven by masculine, pushy principles. Bailey understands and beautifully demonstrates that owning your own power isn't about working harder, making more money, being famous, or whatever other superficial pursuits our society deems as worthy. Instead, she eloquently and compassionately explains that owning your power is about fulfillment, happiness, and loving your life because you create it with intention that is in alignment with your purpose. She strips the fluff and gets to the core. It's truly a heart-centered, compassionate, smart guide designed for women who already have ambition, but want happiness too!"

- **CAROLINE ZWICKSON**, M.A. Counseling Psychology, Women's hormonal balance & life coach

"*Own Your Power* is not just a how-to guide on making your life better; it's a heartfelt confession from Bailey Frumen on how she once put everything on the back burner—her health, her marriage, her life—for her career, only to feel empty and overstressed. Bailey's journey shows her readers that you can have it all—but you must first embrace your beautiful power. Her practical steps will teach you how to own your power, and live a happier life as a result. I recommend this book to any woman who knows she must make a change now to realign her life, energy, health and career so it fits her life's purpose—or risk looking back ten, twenty, or thirty years from now and wondering, 'What was the point of it all?'"

> - **JILL CELESTE, MA**, bestselling author, marketing teacher and founder of the Celestial Marketing Academy

"Women are a powerful force of nature, and yet most of us aren't fully aware of the incredible potential we hold. Many of us are also reluctant to tap into the potency of our gifts as women, mothers, bosses, lovers, creators, movers, and shakers. Bailey brilliantly opens your eyes with a fresh perspective on how to identify your gifts, and your deepest desires and aspirations; by helping you crystallize the clarity of your 'why' in life. This book is a must-read for every woman who dares to live freely according to her will, and be completely fearless in owning her choices, her power and her life. I am gifting this book to my entire tribe!"

> - **MARNELLI MARTIN**, Founder/CEO at Luxe30

"This book helped me realize my blind spots, and how we can find ourselves in an ideal life that feels empty, boring, and lacking in purpose ... even if it looks completely the opposite from the outside. This passage from *Own Your Power* rings so true to me in different stages of my life: '... but the very fact that I believed I was powerless meant that I kept making choices and taking actions that gave away my power.' I think we all can use a roadmap towards designing a truly empowered joyful life. I can't wait to share this book with the women in my life—and a few good men too!"

> - **DOLORES HIRSCHMANN**, Strategist, Speaker, Coach & TEDxOrganizer

"My biggest takeaway from reading *Own Your Power* is that piling on more and more—like more credentials, joining a board, seeking more knowledge, more status, more busy-ness disguised as 'opportunity'—is *not* the path to falling in love with your life! Many of us think that in doing more, we'll find what we love and we'll make the connections we need to make, but that's faulty thinking. We actually need a more sustainable method. I'd absolutely recommend this to any woman who is currently in total overwhelm and can 100 percent relate to Bailey's story. *Own Your Power* will help you to not feel alone, or shameful, or like a loser for doing so much, but yet feeling so underwhelmed about it."

- **LESLIE ZUCKER**, Trainer, Coach, Facilitator & Author of Deliver Workshops That Bring in Clients

"In *Own Your Power*, Bailey Frumen masterfully invites powerful, go-giver women to another level of living life to the fullest. Bailey shares how she had the courage to ask herself a dangerous question—*why?*—and that this simple three-letter word changed her entire life and world. Pursuing our 'why' deeper down the rabbit hole sets the framework for creating a deeply fulfilled life by design, and Bailey walks the reader through an internal, almost alchemical process for transmuting our fear into excitement. Ladies, if you're tired of being stressed and overworked, if you're wondering when it will be 'your turn' to receive the kind of love you give, and if you're ready to finally discover and step into your life purpose, then this is a must-read!"

- **SENSEI VICTORIA WHITFIELD**, author of *Natural Intuition Now*

FOREWORD

Fabienne Fredrickson

We all experience obstacles in our lives.

Challenging situations set us back, or push our buttons. Life often feels like it's coming at us from a hundred different directions. But the biggest obstacles to our success don't come from outside sources: we create them ourselves.

This is great news. Why? Because if our beliefs, mindsets, and choices created an obstacle, they can just as easily un-create it. We just need to acknowledge that we are responsible for our own reality, and *BOOM*, change happens.

I have mentored Bailey Frumen since 2014. I know that she's got a handle on this concept of mindset mastery, because I've witnessed her tremendous growth and expansion. In this book, she will teach you how to stop giving away your power, master your self-talk, get in touch with what you really want, and build a life that speaks to your soul—just as she did for herself.

As Bailey discovered on her personal journey, shifting into a place of personal empowerment is less about doing more stuff and more about stepping back and getting out of your own way. When you let your heart lead you, instead of charging at life head-first, you shift into an entirely new state of being—one from which you can manifest your desires with exponentially more power and ease.

We all get cozy in our comfort zones, even when those comfort zones don't contain the things that truly speak to our souls. In sixteen years of leading boldly with my heart, I've learned that everything you want—and I mean *everything*—is right on the other side of "comfortable."

Successful people—and I don't mean just financially successful, but personally successful as well—are those who do what others are not willing to do. In the case of owning your power, this means delving into the how and why of your present circumstances (whatever they are) and owning those, too. It's a quest for the ages.

So, if you've gotten comfortable being a victim; if you've gotten comfortable sacrificing yourself to your job, or your family; if you've gotten comfortable in the land of "should" and "shouldn't"; it is finally time to let those security blankets fall away and *own your power.*

Within these pages, Bailey gives you tools and techniques to navigate these difficult transitions, set powerful goals, and understand where you've been holding back your own greatness— but, as is always the case with the things that matter, the choice to act is up to you.

The great thing is, you don't have to do it alone. You have Bailey's clarity and wisdom, the tools in this book, and the energetic support of everyone who has ever come to this crossroads in their own lives and moved forward in triumph.

I believe in you. I *know* you've got this.

Are you ready to shift your mindset to one of prosperity, joy, and empowerment? Is it time for you to take a step forward in faith, and claim the power you've always had?

Perfect. Now, turn the page.

With love,

Fabienne Fredrickson
Founder of Boldheart.com, author of *Embrace Your Magnificence: Get Out of Your Own Way and Live a Richer, Fuller, More Abundant Life* and *The Leveraged Mindset*

TABLE *of* CONTENTS

OWN *Your* POWER

"Be the change you wish to see in the world."

\- MAHATMA GANDHI

INTRODUCTION

A woman on a mission is a powerful force of nature. When a woman is connected to her bigger why, her sense of purpose, and her reason for being in the world, she is unstoppable.

Finding that connection isn't always easy: if you are reading this book, you might be feeling stuck, uncertain, or uninspired. **You are in the right place.** I have been where you are, and I have written this book to guide you in identifying obstacles, overcoming fear, and embracing your freedom and your future.

If you are anything like me, you were born a #girlboss, ambitious and driven to excel. But what happens when you reach the top of the corporate ladder and think to yourself, "Now what?" You may be feeling unfulfilled, or not quite as satisfied as you thought you would be.

As ambitious women, we're capable and driven. If you give us a task, it's executed to perfection, on budget and on time. When we were in school, we sat in the front row, completed assignments ahead of time, and even asked if we could do more. But what happens when we don't have a syllabus or a set of guidelines? What happens when we climb to the top of the ladder and think, **"Is *this* what I worked so hard for?"**

If you've ever strived to achieve a goal but crossed the finish line without a sense of deep fulfillment, this book is for you.

I have been where you are and I am going to help illuminate a path to support you in owning your power—lifting the fog to figure out who you really are, what you want, and where you are headed.

How do we find this deeper sense of purpose and fulfillment? My experience is that we have to abandon the rule book and embrace the freedom to create the lives we envision. **I believe that when we are inextricably connected to our why, we are able to be free.** Freedom is a fuel and currency that money cannot buy—it is a state of mind and a choice. Feeling free isn't easy: we often feel held back by long-standing, limiting beliefs. We are tied down to what we think we should be doing, and who we think we should be. This book is about shedding these beliefs to find your why—and with it, your freedom.

MY PATH TO WHY

I've always been driven. I worked hard in school to make honor roll, joined nearly every club, held office on student council, and even participated in community service. But it never felt like it was enough, so I did more.

After completing my Master of Social Work, I dove headfirst into a career, beating out two hundred other applicants for a job as a full-time school social worker. Most people are satisfied with a career like that, and do whatever they can to stay in it for twenty-five years before heading towards retirement. But for me, the job wasn't enough. I went on to pursue my Post-Masters licensure as a Psychotherapist, and I started a private practice while continuing to work full-time at the school. Within six months of opening my new business, I had a two-year waiting list for new clients. I was busy. I worked sixty to seventy hours a week, helping others and putting money in my retirement account.

After seven years at what I thought would be my dream job, I looked around at my life: I had the career, the marriage, the vacations, the house, and the friends that everyone wanted. But I realized something was missing: I didn't feel happy. All I could think was:

"What am I doing here?"

"What's the point?"

"What's my purpose?"

"Why am I here? What is my bigger mission in the world?"

I had no idea. While it looked like I had it all, I felt paralyzed by fear because I didn't know what I wanted. **All I knew was that I didn't want *this*—**the pressure, the stress, feeling stuck, and ultimately feeling unfulfilled in the life that I had worked so hard to create.

I wanted to feel happy, I wanted to feel inspired, powerful, fearless, and most importantly, **I wanted to feel free.** And I couldn't wait until retirement to start enjoying my life.

Have you been there—knowing that you're feeling stuck and that you've got to figure it out, but unsure where to start? For me, that was the scariest part. I was well aware that I wasn't happy, but

I wasn't sure how to move forward.

After months of being stuck, I began a process of change that allowed me to lift the fog from my own life and to find my freedom. After a lot of self-care and self-exploration, I discovered that my purpose in life is to show talented, driven women like me how to own their power and create the lives they truly want. After this revelation, I drew on my own experience to create the Own Your Power Program. I quit my job, and ever since, I've dedicated my time helping women feel free to play bigger, live bigger, love bigger, and believe that they can share their mission and vision in the world with confidence.

Many of my clients have come to me from a place of uncertainty. They know that they are feeling stuck and want to make a change, but they don't know where to start. They feel ready to transform their lives, to begin discovering their bigger missions in the world—but they are unsure of how to take the first step. My purpose in my Own Your Power Program, and in this book, is to help women take concrete, manageable steps towards their purpose and their freedom.

WHAT NOW?

This book is a jumping-off point to help you begin to feel powerful, fearless, and free—all by learning how to confidently own your power. The days of feeling paralyzed by uncertainty are over. This book will be your opportunity to start listening to yourself. I've shared stories of my own transformation as well as the stories of the many women I have worked with. Most chapters include a "case study" from a client, giving you a real-life example of how a woman used these tools to transform her life. Each chapter of this book is designed to help you tackle an obstacle or to take a new step. As the book progresses, I will show you how to uncover what has been holding you back, how to release fear, and most importantly, I will show you exactly how to own your power by creating a specific vision for your future and then taking action towards achieving your goals.

You've got big things to do in the world. It's time to get clear about what has been holding you back, and figure out what you want and who you are meant to be.

Are you ready to get started?

"Forget what we became;
what matters is what we've become,
and our potential to overcome."

- ANIEKEE TOCHUKWU EZEKIEL

CHAPTER ONE

Finding Your Freedom

I have always been ambitious.

Until I was twenty-nine, this meant taking on as much responsibility as I could. I thought working as hard as possible and helping others would help me get ahead in my career and find personal fulfillment. My efforts in high school, college, and my MSW program culminated in the busiest period of my life: working full-time as a school counselor while maintaining a private psychotherapy practice.

From the first day of my career, I saw early retirement as my end goal. I loved my job, but looked forward to the day when I would be in charge of my own time. I thought working more would get me to retirement quicker: if I put twenty-five years into the grind, I would finally have the expansive freedom to do whatever I pleased, and to enjoy myself and start living.

I was used to working hard, and willingly gave up my pleasure, play, or free time because I thought doing so meant getting ahead and making an impact. When I started working at the school, my days were filled with meetings and classroom observations. I could have had my weekends, evenings, and summers off, but my belief that I could and should do more was deeply ingrained.

So I started my private practice. Practically overnight, I was busy. *Very* busy.

As it turns out, I was not alone in working well beyond forty hours each week. As Facebook COO Sheryl Sandberg shared in her wildly popular book, *Lean In,* A survey of high-earning professionals in the corporate world found that 62 percent work more than fifty hours a week, and 10 percent work more than eighty hours per week.

Working sixty or more hours each week, I gave up a lot. I didn't have time for yoga, or for grabbing wine with my girlfriends. My husband and I were on a first-name basis with the Chinese food delivery guy. Despite these realities, I thought to myself: *"I've made it, right? Isn't this what I wanted?"*

I knew that my life looked great from the outside, too. I had a beautiful home, a handsome husband, and two cute dogs. Because I worked so much, I had plenty of money in the bank.

But despite how I thought I should feel, one idea kept creeping in: I was starting to lose me.

I began to have panic attacks for the first time in my life. At 2:00 a.m., my eyes would blink open and I would find myself in a sweat, almost unable to breathe, my heart pounding in my chest. In the middle of the night, my racing mind filled with questions:

"What am I doing?"

"Is this what I want?"

"If it isn't—then what do I really want?"

I felt both out of control and completely stuck. I was a counselor, someone who helped other people to deal with anxiety, panic attacks, and self-doubt. I didn't understand why this was happening to me. I had always done the right thing, hadn't I? I had always been in control of my life, hadn't I?

So why did I feel so powerless?

The panic attacks progressed. They began to strike while I was driving, forcing me to pull to the side of the road until they passed. I had no idea what to do.

It took me a while to admit that I needed help. Stressed out, overwhelmed, and exhausted, I finally went to a doctor. She concluded that I was suffering from adrenal fatigue. This syndrome commonly occurs when someone is overtaxing herself and is not making enough time for self-care.

The doctor recommended supplements and acupuncture to help my symptoms—but she stressed that the most important thing of all for me to do was *slow down*.

I wanted to laugh. If I slowed down, who would be counselor to my students, therapist to my clients, wife to my husband? Who would do everything I did in a day?

As I drove home from that appointment, I realized that I didn't know how to slow down. **The truth was this: I was taking care of everyone but myself.** I had been going at a breakneck pace for as long as I could remember. Suddenly, though, I didn't remember why.

Why had I taken on so many responsibilities? *Why* was I filling my days with work, leaving no time for myself? I no longer had any idea.

MY AH-HA MOMENT

I would love to say that everything magically improved after that doctor's visit; that I figured out how to slow down and care for myself. But that's not what happened. Really, I didn't change much. I took the supplements, I went to acupuncture, but I didn't figure out how to make the big changes that would answer the questions that plagued me.

I continued to have panic attacks. I continued to wonder what I was doing wrong and how I could improve things. And I continued to work nonstop, because I didn't have the answers, and the easiest thing was to just keep doing what I knew how to do: *work.*

A few months later, a client canceled her session; finally, I was able to fit a yoga class into my busy schedule. As I lay on my mat for meditation I heard the instructor recite a quote by Ralph Waldo Emerson: *"A man is what he thinks about all day long."*

Was this true? Each day, all I thought about was how stressed and overwhelmed I was feeling. I realized that this quote was all too real for me—I felt out of control in my own life.

This simple quote set me on the path of self-discovery and change. If I didn't want to feel out of control, I had to figure out how I *did* want to feel. I had to start getting clear about what I really wanted my life to look and feel like. How did I want to spend my days, months, and years?

Finally, I came to a conclusion:

IT WAS TIME TO OWN MY POWER.

I was done with feeling powerless, out-of-control, and unhappy. I was ready to make the changes I needed to feel free and empowered in my own life.

SHEDDING FEAR

Back then, I knew that what I was doing—working to exhaustion, feeling stressed, and also feeling bored—wasn't working. Anytime I wanted to achieve a goal or accomplish a task, I would muscle my way through it by pushing, working hard, and stopping at nothing until I got what I wanted. Unfortunately, I was beginning to realize that my "old way" of doing things wasn't going to work to help me find a "new way" to live my life feeling fulfilled and free.

But I was stuck: I was still attached to the idea that I *needed* to stay on the career path I'd envisioned in my early twenties, the path that my hard work in school had prepared me for. With this belief in place, I felt powerless to figure out how to change my life—**but the very fact that I believed I was powerless meant that I kept making choices and taking actions that gave away my power.**

It was a vicious cycle, and unless I made a drastic change, it would never end.

I knew that things had to change, but I was scared because I didn't know how to change them. As an ambitious woman, I was accustomed to living life in the driver's seat. But when I hit a wall, I felt stuck, uncertain, and overwhelmed as to what to do next. I was used to feeling in control, so the uncertainty that settled in when I realized I needed to change was scary.

This is the case for many women. In our pursuit of freedom and fulfillment, we chase the careers we thought we always wanted, and scale mountains of obstacles, only to be left wondering …

… Now what?

... **What's my next step?**

... **What do I want?**

... **How can I live a bigger, more fulfilling life?**

... **How can I give more in this life?**

... **How can I make a bigger impact?**

Maybe you're there right now: you know you feel stuck, and that you need to make a change, but you're not sure where to begin. Maybe you're afraid of what might happen if you shift direction.

Without the answers to the above questions, even the most vibrant and "go-getting" women become filled with fear. We feel stagnant and unable to figure out who we are and what we are meant to do in this life.

With my decision to own my power, I finally shed my fear and stepped towards my bigger purpose.

STEPS TOWARDS CLARITY

Trying to rewrite my whole way of living seemed like a daunting task, but I knew that I needed to give myself permission to take the time to lift the fog and to get clear about the life I wanted to live. I decided to make a change by thinking about transformation in manageable pieces.

My transformative experience in yoga class reminded me how important physical health is to well-being, and I knew one essential step was taking better care of myself.

I started by creating my ideal vision for a healthy life. I set goals: first, I would be sure to get enough exercise. (For me, this meant regularly attending yoga classes and going on occasional runs to boost my energy.) In addition, I would be sure to get seven or eight hours of sleep each night—enough to enjoy nourishing rest, to wake up feeling replenished, and to make it through the day without feeling exhausted. Finally, I would make sure my diet supported my energy and my mental clarity: I incorporated more fruits and veggies, and resolved to drink more water.

After taking these steps towards physical health, I had the support in place to sort through the complex emotions that came with accepting change into my life. I was ready to move towards transformations in all other areas of my life: emotional well-being, relationships, career and finance, and spirituality.

As I considered my emotional well-being, I knew it was vital to stop judging myself. I didn't have it all figured out yet, but the opportunity to make real change was something to be thankful for. I needed to give myself permission to take a pause, to take care of my body and my emotional well-being, and to seek for answers only when I had the mental clarity I needed. Letting go of expectations about what I *should* be doing brought me one step closer to my answers.

Once I let go of my judgments, I finally came to a powerful realization: **I wanted to fall in love with my life—a life that only *I* had the power to create.**

I wanted to feel connected to the work I did each day. This meant re-considering how I would spend my time in order to make room for that life.

I took a serious look at my job and finances, and asked myself once more:

"Is this what I really want?"

"What's my purpose?"

"Why am I here?"

"What is my bigger mission in the world?"

These questions no longer felt overwhelming. Instead, they were exciting.

I thought about the fulfillment I got from my job at the school and from my private practice. I had always known I was born to help others, but I didn't feel like I was fulfilling my purpose; I was still waiting for my bigger calling.

I also realized that I couldn't wait until retirement to fall in love with my life. I was good at my job, but it didn't give me the freedom I needed to take care of others and myself. It didn't allow me to enjoy each day. Soon after this realization, I sat in my bosses' office and gave my resignation.

As I grew more confident in my own vision and began to own my power, the fog lifted from my life and my mission in the world became evident. I am here to help other ambitious women fall in love with their lives—to help them find clarity and greater connection to their purposes.

With my background in counseling, as well as my newfound sense of empowerment and freedom, I knew I was in an ideal position to help other women get unstuck. I could help women take the action needed to live lives they love. This is when I created my **Own Your Power Program.**

These steps led me towards a life I fully embrace each day: empowering women is my why, not just my job but my spiritual calling. I am finally in love with my life.

As you move through the chapters in this book, you'll begin the process of creating a life you will love—starting with the process of **getting unstuck**.

"Sometimes, the questions are complicated and the answers are simple."

- DR. SEUSS

CHAPTER TWO

Getting Unstuck

Just because you've decided to change doesn't mean that you will.

It's a little tough love, but a lesson I had to learn the hard way. When I made up my mind to change my life, I expected it to happen immediately. I was used to getting what I wanted quickly through hard work. When I didn't experience immediate change, I began to feel disappointed and to judge myself—I felt like a failure. Unsurprisingly, my self-judgment didn't help me move forward. In fact, it made me even more stuck and resistant to change.

I'm here to tell you that it doesn't have to be so hard. In fact, I'm going to give you the shortcut to getting unstuck.

If you're used to getting what you want through dedication and diligence, you might expect change to come to you as easily and quickly as the other things you've achieved. When change doesn't happen right away, you might begin to feel frustrated or sad. However, the judgments you make about yourself and your progress only cause you to become more stuck in your old ways.

Why? Because in order to feel fearless, powerful, and free, we need to travel a new path. Trying to forge a new path using our old methodologies does not work. **Remember: Just because you've decided to change doesn't mean that you will.**

In this chapter, we will:

- Learn why the "shoulds" in our lives keep us stuck, and how to get over them
- Examine our self-talk for clues about what's keeping us stuck
- Take our first steps toward changing unhelpful beliefs

When you are ready to invite lasting change into your life, it's time for a new way. Instead of arduous work, we're going to use ease and flow. Instead of powering through to achieve our goals, we're going to *feel* our way through to achieve our visions.

Sound good? I thought so!

GETTING OVER THE "SHOULDS"

The truth is this: what keeps us stuck is "should." We often get caught up in living the life that we think we "should" be living, instead of the life we really want.

Maybe you've heard a little voice in your head say …

... *I* should *go for that job*
(even though I'm not excited about it)

... *I* should *go to that school*
(even though I'm not sure it's the one for me)

... *I* should *date that guy*
(even though I like someone else)

... *I* should *say yes*
(even though I don't want to)

When this little voice comes into your head, begin to ask yourself a new set of questions:

... *Have I been doing what I think I* should *be doing,*
(or what I actually want to do?)

... *Have I been the person others think I* should *be,*
(or the person I really am?)

Many of my clients come to me doing the job they believe they *should* be doing, and saying yes to "opportunities" that they *should* be excited about. They want to change, are stuck in those preconceived notions of who, what, where, and when.

Sometimes our whole lives are built around ideas of who we *should* be, not who we want to be. In all these cases, living in the "should" drains us and puts us farther from our authentic paths. When we make choices and decisions dictated by what we think we should be doing, we rob ourselves of the opportunity to connect with the lives that we truly want.

Living in the "should" allows us to tune out and disconnect from our desires. It's easier to look around at what everyone else is doing, and use their behavior as a barometer, than to actually ask ourselves what we want. It's easier to look outside than to look within—but that's exactly what we have to do in order to own our power and reclaim our true selves.

Asking ourselves what we want can be terrifying. There are so many deep questions we avoid ...

... What do I really want?

... What message do I want to share?

... What is my bigger purpose and mission in the world?

If we don't take the time to stop and ask ourselves these questions, we don't give ourselves the opportunity to listen to the answers.

We grow in direct correlation to the depth of the questions that we ask ourselves. When we live in the "should," we fill up the space that we could use to explore what we really want with mindless tasks and to-dos. We never ask those deeper questions.

Heavy stuff, huh? It doesn't have to be.

This book is your opportunity to answer the questions that make you sweat and keep you up at night. This book will not change you by osmosis. Instead, it has been designed as a conversation. I want to not only provide for you a new way of thinking, but also give you the tools to make real and lasting changes in your life.

TAKING YOUR FIRST STEP

You know in your heart that you were meant for bigger things, but you simply don't know how to get there. So what's holding you back?

Let's start with what it sounds like to be in your head:

... I don't know what my purpose is.

... People are going to laugh if I share my vision.

... What I want is small/silly/not important enough, and it's not going to make a difference.

... Who am I to think that I have something special to share?

I'm going to ask you a hard question: **who are you *not* to show up and shine? Who are you not to share your strengths and talents with others?**

When we are ready to share our bigger mission and vision with the world, we have two big obstacles to overcome. The first obstacle is our self-talk. As human beings, it is all too easy to talk ourselves out of shining. But self-talk can be used to positive ends, too: just as we can convince ourselves we aren't worthy, we can change our perspectives and decide that it is our time to share our gifts with the world.

If you want to own your power and be unstoppable, you need to master your self-talk—starting right now. As you complete the writing exercise for this chapter, let go of any negative self-judgment. Dream big. See how it feels to let yourself fly free without your inner critic dragging you down.

The second obstacle to overcome when you are ready to own your power is your *belief system.* Our beliefs about who we are and what we are capable of can stand in the way of greatness.

This book was designed to help you identify the blocks and obstacles that are standing in your way, to get clear about your belief systems (and change them if they are not working for you), and to take action in order to live fearlessly and share your purpose in the world.

Throughout this book you will find opportunities to reflect on your way of life and your belief systems. I encourage you to pace yourself while reading. Don't devour the book; read it one chapter at a time. After each chapter, put the book down and give yourself a few days to look at and experience the world through a new set of eyes and a new, empowered belief system.

OWN YOUR POWER: REFLECTION

If I felt free to be me, what would I do, be, and experience in the world?

_____

_____

_____

_____

_____

_____

_____

How will choosing what *I* want make a difference in my life?

_____

_____

_____

_____

_____

_____

What self-talk comes up when I envision my ideal life?

_____

_____

_____

_____

_____

_____

OWN YOUR POWER TIP

I often tell my clients: Don't lose sight of your vision in service of the "how."

What does this mean? Don't get stuck thinking "How am I going to make this happen?" A focus on "how" can lead you to censor and self-edit.

When we get stuck in the "how" of things—like, "How am I going to pay for this?" or "How will I make the time to do that?"—it puts us in a place of judgment and shut-down; we prevent ourselves from growth and openness to possibility.

Set "how" aside for now, and allow yourself the space to explore. The truth is that nothing changes in our lives if we don't give ourselves the space to grow and dream.

HOW JULIE GOT UNSTUCK

Working with Bailey has given me the courage to start making some big changes in my life. We worked together to dream up my ideal lifestyle; Bailey pushed me to realize that everything I want is possible— and more. She taught me that getting my toes wet and taking small steps towards my dreams everyday is what leads to major growth. I have a newfound clarity about what I want and a roadmap of how to make it happen.

Before working with Bailey, I was stuck in a cycle of fear and "perfection paralysis." I was scared to make any changes in my life because I was always worried about whether I would measure up to my own high expectations, so I stalled and did nothing instead.

Once we started working together in the Own Your Power Program, I realized that these unrealistic expectations were holding me back. If I wanted to become "unstuck," all I needed to do was re-frame my thoughts and determine why I wanted to make these changes. Allowing myself the space to make one small change at a time was huge—this is how all great changes are made! Once I started moving in the direction of my goals, my vision became clear.

Working with Bailey allowed me to remove the nagging pressure and high expectations of myself that were ultimately holding me back. I was able to take control of not just my business ideas, but each different area of my life. I determined what my ideal outcome would be, and Bailey was able to help me break that down into actionable steps and goals. We worked together to create a list of champagne-celebration-worthy milestones that includes a blog launch, a yoga retreat, and travel to Thailand!

-**Julie O'Brien**, *Holistic Health Coach, Colorado*

*"Life begins
at the edge of your fears."*

- MATSHONA DHLIWAYO

CHAPTER THREE

Release Fear

There are four important steps to owning your power: **releasing fear, (re)writing your story, creating your vision, and taking action.**

To make lasting change in your life, you have to look at what stands in your way. Most often, fear is our biggest obstacle, which is why it's the first and most important step in this process. In order to own our power and achieve our goals, we need to be clear about what has been holding us back.

In this chapter, we will:

- Identify roadblocks that keep you stuck
- Examine recurring patterns that just don't work
- Discover the negative belief systems that need to hit the road

We need to identify where our fear is coming from. Sometimes it is easier to see what fear is blocking us from doing than to figure out the origin or root cause of the fear. It is important to get at the root cause—which are often negative and disempowering belief systems. However, before we go all the way to the root, we will focus on the way that fear crops up in our day-to-day life, and how it holds us back.

The first step to releasing fear is observing when and how you experience fear. What triggers your fear response? Work? Health? Relationship status? Friends or family?

Where is your fear? Where is your resistance?

Think about that big idea or desire that has been calling to you—perhaps a big leap you're just dying to take, or maybe a transition that feels almost inevitable.

Then, ask yourself,

"Why haven't I acted yet?"

We've all got excuses:

> ... *It's too expensive, I can't afford it.*
> ... *I'm really busy.*
> ... *I'll do it later.*

We've got doubts:

> ... *I'm not good enough.*
> ... *Who wants to listen to me?*
> ... *I don't know where to start.*

We've got what-if's:

> *... What if I fail?*
> *... What if it doesn't work?*
> *... What if I'm not sure what I want it to look like?*

If your what-ifs, doubts, and excuses aren't working for you anymore, it's time to own your power. You can be free of all the gunk that has held you back and kept you playing small.

You can be free of your fear.

Playing small doesn't serve you. When you hold back from following your deepest desires, you won't feel fulfilled. Playing small keeps you stuck. I invite you to take your hopes and desires off the shelf and dream a bigger dream.

I invite you to acknowledge that only you have the power to create freedom and a life on your own terms.

When it comes to releasing fear, be prepared to think differently, to look at things a bit differently, and to radically shift your life in the direction of your dreams...here we go!

OWN YOUR POWER: REFLECTION

What has been holding you back from reaching your goals?

_____

_____

_____

_____

_____

Can you identify where fear and resistance are triggered in your life?

_____

_____

_____

_____

_____

_____

OBSERVING & CATCHING

Once you have identified the places where fear is holding you back, you will be ready to further explore the negative beliefs that keep you from shining your brightest.

According to the Laboratory of Neuro Imaging at the University of Southern California, the average person has about 48.6 thoughts per minute. That adds up to between 20,000 and 70,000 thoughts per day. Further research shows that up to 80 percent of our thoughts are negative. These negative beliefs are often at the root of our fears, causing us to feel inadequate, incapable, or just too scared to move forward.

At the start of any transition or transformation, it is essential to let go of what no longer serves you. This leaves you ready to accept the good stuff that awaits you on the road ahead. As you take the time to truly examine your belief systems, look at the messages that no longer work for you. Often, the best way to identify our negative beliefs is to see what they have held us back from. When you observe that your negative beliefs are standing between where you are now and where you hope to be, you know it's time to change.

I developed a process called Observing & Catching™ to help you create this change. In this process, it is essential to first "observe and catch" a negative belief or feeling as it arises. I use the word "observe" because to observe means to acknowledge but remain unchanged by.

If you were on safari, you would observe the giraffes, lions, and other animals from a distance, and would not interact with them. Thus, your behavior would not change, and neither would theirs.

Observing & Catching is a process of removing yourself from the intensity of a negative emotion. When a negative belief or feeling presents itself, "catch" it. Don't let the feeling permeate you or impact your self-talk. Instead, decide that you are going to "catch" the feeling and hold it at arm's length. For example, rather than thinking "I am angry," observe the emotion that comes up, and try to recognize it as what it is, a feeling. Say to yourself "I feel angry" and stop the feeling in its tracks before it permeates you. **Remember that this is a temporary state, not who you are.**

Once you've caught the negative belief or feeling, observe what comes up for you while trying to remain unchanged. Don't interact with your feeling right away: don't judge yourself, and don't run away from your experience. Just let your feeling be in its "natural habitat," and watch what it does. Now that you're able to hold the feeling at arm's length, you can also consider why it came up in the first place.

The power in Observing & Catching is that you stay in the driver's seat. You have more control over how you feel and are not thrown off-kilter by every negative thought, belief, or feeling that you experience.

These exercises might seem very uncomfortable at first. No one really wants to sit with their own stuff, but it's necessary to master this process in order to truly benefit from the next steps on the road ahead. So, before you move on to the next section, practice Observing and Catching your negative beliefs until you're comfortable with the process.*

MOVING ON

Now that you've gotten comfortable Observing & Catching your negative feelings and fear responses, it's time to examine them more closely. So roll up your sleeves, dig out the tissues, and get ready to dive deep into making your new belief systems stick.

Full disclosure and warning: This could get messy.

I lovingly give this warning from a place of understanding and "been there, done that." I've done this exercise, gotten frustrated, cried, felt totally overwhelmed, gave up, and then went back to it again. My own difficult but transformative experience makes me feel that it's only fair to give warning.

When we want to move a mountain, we often need to start by digging away at the rocks at its foot. First we move the small rocks, and then the boulders—until finally we are ready to move the mountain itself.

In this case, the "rocks" are the disempowering belief systems that keep us afraid and hold us back from owning our power. So, use this opportunity to reflect on the disempowering beliefs that you carry around and that stand in the way of your best life.

In the space below, brainstorm all of the disempowering beliefs that you hold. Try to do this from a place of love; let your beliefs flow free without any judgment.

*For more resources and videos on exactly how to use the process of Observing & Catching, visit **OwnYourPowerBookBonuses.com**

OWN YOUR POWER: REFLECTION

What are the negative belief systems that you've been carrying around?

_____

_____

_____

_____

_____

_____

What is the hardest part about identifying your negative belief systems?

_____

_____

_____

_____

_____

Sometimes, the hardest part of the "tough stuff" is being honest and non-judgmental. It's difficult not to be critical of ourselves. You wrote down some of your self-talk in Chapter Two, and we'll return to this topic again in Chapter Four and throughout the book. For now, continue to keep in mind that when we stop judging ourselves, it's easier to uncover our blocks and to create space to grow. This is an important lesson to learn.

When you are ready, start to think about how your might transform your negative beliefs. Many times, we feel like our "stuff" is what holds us back from happiness. While that might be true in some cases, I want you to dig a little deeper underneath.

Look at your list of negative beliefs and use this as a magic-wand opportunity to start to uncover how you would rather feel and what you would rather believe to be true about yourself and your path ahead.

OWN YOUR POWER: REFLECTION

If I waved my magic wand, life would look like ...

_____

_____

_____

_____

_____

Belief systems are a difficult structure to tackle. They are truly the mainframe that keeps everything functioning (or not functioning) in our lives. Negative belief systems can affect just about everything in our world, from how we see ourselves, to how capable we think we are, and to what we believe that we deserve.

The good news is that we have the power to change belief systems that are no longer working for us.

Here's how to change them.

CHANGING YOUR BELIEFS

Step 1: Identify the disempowering beliefs that keep you stuck and fearful. These are often the roadblocks and obstacles to your success. Using the chart below, I encourage you to use the left-hand column to brainstorm the beliefs that have felt like the biggest blocks in your life.

Step 2: Listen to your soul. What do these beliefs keep you from cultivating in your life? Here is another way to think about it: if you were to wake up tomorrow without these beliefs, what would your life look like? For example, if your disempowering belief is, *"I'll never figure out what I am supposed to do with my life,"* it's holding you back from a lot: *"Feeling successful, making a bigger impact in the world, sharing my passion and unique gifts with the world."*

Step 3: Use what you truly want to bring into your life as fuel to create an empowering new belief. In our example from above, our empowering new belief might be, *"I can be open to the opportunity to listen to myself and I can uncover what has held me back from figuring out my purpose."* As you can see, the effectiveness of this exercise isn't in trying to change your belief systems completely—you won't begin to believe the opposite of what you've believed so far. Rather, you will know that you have the power to shift from a place of disempowerment into the driver's seat of change.

Now, it's time to work through your own belief systems.

OWN YOUR POWER: REFLECTION

NEGATIVE/ DISEMPOWERING BELIEF	WHAT THIS BELIEF HOLDS ME BACK FROM HAVING IN MY LIFE	POSITIVE/ EMPOWERING BELIEF
Example: I'll never find my soul mate, no one is ever going to want me, I'm going to be alone forever.	Satisfaction within myself, having a meaningful connection, being present, enjoying my life now	I can be present and have fun in my life *right now*. I can trust that I will have a partner in the future who deserves me

It might take you a few tries to recognize your negative beliefs for what they are. These structures are deeply rooted, and frame how you see yourself and the world around you. But when your beliefs are no longer serving you, they keep you afraid of making the changes you need to move forward on your path. It's time to transform these beliefs bit-by-bit.

Each time a negative belief pops into your head, that's your cue to replace it with the empowering new belief you've written down.

HOW ISABEL FOUND FREEDOM FROM FEAR

Working with Bailey helped me to get clear about what I wanted to do and where I want to go next in many areas of my life. I had been feeling very stuck in my career, with my finances, and with my health. My default mode was to feel overwhelmed. I self-medicated with food, and I felt powerless and helpless.

Bailey became my accountability partner, cheerleader, taskmaster, big sister, sympathetic ear, and all-around supporter!

She was all of this while remaining compassionate and administering gentle but tough love when needed. I felt comfortable sharing my deepest, darkest fears with Bailey because she made me feel very comfortable from the start. I have gained a new filter to view my challenges as opportunities for growth. Now, I hold the power and confidence to decide whether any given opportunity would be a step forward towards my vision or a diversion or side mission worth exploring.

In less than a year, I have opened up opportunities for moving forward in my career and increasing my income. I am also much wiser about strategizing my time and removing barriers to my productivity. I am excited and hopeful for the future. Thank you, Bailey!

— **Isabel Veguilla**, *Graphic Designer & Educational Applications Specialist*

"Life isn't about finding yourself. Life is about creating yourself."

~GEORGE BERNARD SHAW

CHAPTER FOUR

(Re)Write Your Story

Remember when I shared that we have nearly 70,000 thoughts each day? If these thoughts are positive, we will feel unstoppable in achieving our goals. However, when we are feeling stuck, the negative thoughts that loom in our heads can hold us back from owning our power and living our best lives.

In my own journey, the hardest step was taking charge of my thoughts and accepting that only I had the power to (re)write my story. I was sure that all 70,000 of my thoughts were random and impossible to control. I didn't know that my thoughts were incredibly influential: negative thoughts held me back from my power and from the life I wanted to create. At first, I felt powerless to change my life. It wasn't until I discovered the tools I share in this book that I felt like I could really shift my mindset and take charge of my life.

The truth is that we become what we believe; we become what we think about. I came to embrace the Emerson quote I shared in the introduction: "A man is what he thinks about all day long." If you constantly think that you are powerless to change your life, you will remain powerless. However, the good news is that you have the power to change the script in your head.

In this chapter, we'll focus on the second step to owning your power—(re)writing your story. Limiting and negative beliefs can permeate all elements of your life, from your self-image to how you interact with others. You know that negative beliefs can hold you back from action; now, you'll learn how to step into your most powerful mindset by changing the script and shifting your beliefs to serve you instead of standing in your way.

In this chapter, we will:

- Identify recurring negative self-talk patterns
- Examine how our self-talk impacts our feelings and behaviors
- Discover how to shift our mindset and beliefs to change the script

Did you know that self-talk is the #1 determining factor as to whether you will become someone who feels confident or someone who feels powerless? As you take the time to ask yourself to truly examine your script, look at the messages that are no longer working for you. The best way to identify our negative self-talk is to examine what we wouldn't ever say out loud about someone else. These are the things we say to ourselves (consciously or unconsciously) that we would never say to a best friend, a sister, or even a co-worker. Why do we say these things to ourselves, sometimes over and over again? It's time to change the script.

THE SELF-TALK CYCLE

As my clients can attest, getting acquainted with the self-talk cycle is a game changer. Learning how the self-talk cycle works illuminates what holds us back. Once you see what isn't working, you can begin to change the script and (re)write your story.

Once we are able to clearly see how our self-talk influences just about every feeling we have and every action we take, we realize that simple shifts in our mindset can have BIG results.

This exercise is a favorite of mine and one that I continue to use nearly every day to keep myself on track. **The Self-Talk Cycle is an unbelievably powerful tool to help you to shift your mindset from one that operates at a deficit (feeling less than or not enough) to one that comes from a place of abundance and flow.**

Here's how it works:

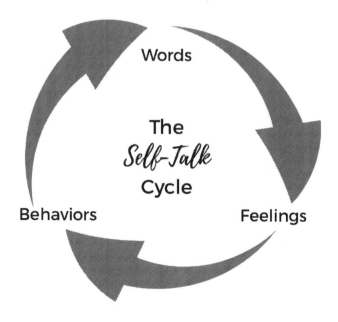

The *Self-Talk* Cycle

Words

Feelings

Behaviors

Our *words* (internal dialogue) affect the way we *feel* about ourselves, others, experiences, and even the world around us. In many ways, our words are the blueprint by which we live our life. Our words control our story and thereby our perception of our experiences and interactions.

Our *feelings* in turn affect and influence our *behavior.* When our self-talk is positive and upbeat, we feel happy, fearless, and free; therefore, we take chances. Our confidence allows us to take the necessary actions to achieve our goals. On the other side of the coin, if our internal dialogue is negative and disempowering, then we will feel incapable and therefore experience resistance to action. This holds us back from the lives we want.

For example …

Our *behavior* includes our actions, both positive and negative. When we think about making a change, our mind typically moves straight to our behavior: we want to change how we act in the external world. But sometimes that means we forget about the shift that needs to happen in our self-talk and feelings in order to make long-term, lasting changes to our patterns of behavior.

Just as positive words beget positive feelings and actions, negative self-talk leads to negative feelings and negative behaviors—or inaction. Because the self-talk cycle is a continuous loop, it will not stop until you decide to make a change.

As Dr. Peter Gray, research professor at Boston College, highlighted in his 2014 TED talk, our self-talk and self-concept is largely determined by whether we feel powerful or powerless in enacting change in our life. As you can see from the examples on the next page, if **our self-talk is negative, our feelings are negative, and our behavior/actions are negative.** Rarely would we ever find a case where being judgmental and hard on yourself results in positive behaviors, feelings, or actions.

CHANGING THE SCRIPT

Using the self-talk cycle below, identify your negative thoughts, feelings, and actions on the left and then use the self-talk cycle on the right to shift your script.

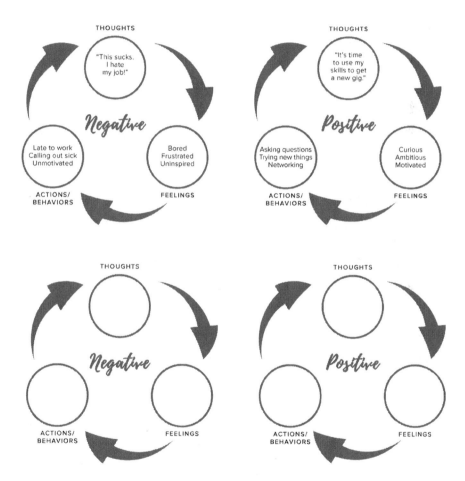

Making the shift into positive self-talk takes a tremendous amount of practice. You are essentially rewriting the script, creating new thought patterns, and re-programming your brain. This shift in your mindset can take some serious heavy lifting, and may be difficult at times. Hold onto this truth as you work at changing your script.

When you acknowledge that you have the power to rewrite the story of your life, you may feel both excited and overwhelmed.

While we feel excited at the possibility of change, we can also feel a bit daunted by the focus and determination it takes to stay consistent in transforming our self-talk cycles. I promise you this: just like anything else that you've learned in your lifetime—from multiplication to riding a bike—it becomes easier with practice.

THE NEW STORY: AFFIRMATIONS

We often like things that come easily to us, whether it's from a natural talent or ability, or something we've practiced so much that it has become second nature. When things come easily, it produces specific feeling—affirmation. Affirmations are easy to come by when what we're faced with isn't that hard. For example, after cleaning and organizing your desk, you tend to step back, exhale, and think, "good job!"

Changing your self-talk might not come easily, so it's important to have a plan in place to deal with any negative judgments that might come up as you work on re-writing your story.

The next step in re-writing the script is to provide yourself with a new outlook to support the positive shift in your self-talk.

Here's how it works: our words make a BIG difference in how we impact the world. Think about it: if you say to a colleague/friend, "I really like your outfit," they tend to stand a little taller and smile a bit more. Pretty simple.

Since we know the impact of our words on others, **we can use our words to make a BIG difference on how we show up in the world**. If you look in the mirror and say, "Wow, I love this scarf, it makes me feel powerful" before speaking in front of a group of fifty people, you are far more likely to rock your speech than if you were to look in the mirror and say, "I look frumpy again. Oh, well." Your words impact you as they would a colleague or friend—but even more strongly.

In the experience of life, we get messages from other people all day, every day. The only power we have to get what we need in order to feel good is to give it to ourselves. We cannot control the words and message from other people, positive or negative. Most often, when someone is unkind, impatient, or cruel to us, it has much more to do with their self-talk and their story than it has to do with us. For better or worse, we cannot control others. That being said, we have the power to control how the words of others impact us. This is why it is important to make a consistent effort to build yourself up and celebrate what makes you unique, powerful, and impactful.

CELEBRATING YOURSELF

It is very common that we focus on the 2 percent of what's difficult rather than celebrate the 98 percent of what is going well in our lives. As ambitious and driven women, we tend to criticize, critique, and judge before giving ourselves the high-five for a job well done. The success we experience in life comes from highlighting and capitalizing on our strengths. The best way to experience this success consistently is to celebrate your wins.

I want to know—What are you good at? What makes you exceptional and special? How do you stand out from the crowd? We've all got that certain something special about us, here's your opportunity to brag.

OWN YOUR POWER: REFLECTION

Create a list of all the great ways that you show up in the world.

What is awesome about you?

_____

_____

_____

_____

_____

_____

_____

What do people often compliment you for?

_____

_____

_____

_____

_____

How have you made an impact on the world?

_____

_____

_____

_____

_____

**What are your top three favorite affirmations
from the list above?**

1. _____

_____

2. _____

_____

3. _____

_____

Now that you've written down your affirmations, come back to them whenever you need to change the course of your self-talk. As soon as you observe negative thoughts coming to mind—or experience negative feelings or observe unhelpful actions—try to change your self-talk right away. You might be surprised to find how quickly your feelings and behaviors shift, too.

WHEN IT CLICKED FOR MARISKA

I consider myself extraordinarily lucky to have been able to work with Bailey.

Let me preface this by saying that I made a massive mistake in hiring a business coach earlier in the year; that experience really didn't gel with me. It was quite awful and I spent thousands of dollars only to find myself back where I started. I had lost a lot of faith in coaching, even though I am a coach myself.

I really needed the nurturing and kind, yet inspiring and firm belief in myself that Bailey gave me. She is incredible, and always made me feel beautifully supported – not only that, she treated me like a winner when I had allowed myself to sink into being a victim. When I took the steps we'd mapped out together, things started to bloom in my own coaching business.

Before working with Bailey, I was losing faith in myself, I was blocked from writing, and I was really almost unable to step into my role as a coach. Then I received Bailey's gentle kick in the butt! Amazing—when I followed the advice that Bailey and I had discussed would be a great (and aligned) plan to get me going again…. things just started to fall into place and my coaching blossomed.

I really lost my "being a victim" B.S. entirely once I started with what we'd mapped out, and things just started to happen. I got published in the Huffington Post – so obviously I got over my writer's block! I got twenty-five one-off session clients in the space of three weeks (and they adore what I'm doing, and more are coming in) and am in the process of signing long-term clients now.

Bailey, you truly set me on fire. I know it took me a wee while to apply our plan, but once I did, I've flown, and I am so grateful for you, and to you.

— **Mariska Andersen, PhD,** *writer and coach at MariskaAnderson.com*

DENISE CHANGED HER MINDSET

Before I began coaching with Bailey, I felt very confused and kind of lost as to how to go about changing my mindset and finding work that I love. I really struggled with what I truly wanted in life. In coaching with Bailey, things have definitely shifted. I feel much more optimistic and have made more moves towards the life I want. Even in this short time that we've worked together, she has changed my life for the better. I am so thankful to have found her!

— **Denise Del Russo,** *Make-up Artist at DeniseDelRusso. com and editor-at-large at LiveTheGlamour.com*

"If you don't know where you're going, you will probably end up somewhere else."

~LAURENCE J. PETER

CHAPTER FIVE

Vision

What would your life look like if you weren't affected by feeling the way that you do?

As you learned early on in this book, there are four important steps to owning your power: **releasing fear, (re)writing your story, creating your vision,** and **taking action.**

We have set the stage for transformation by creating a solid foundation. We began by identifying our limiting beliefs to let go of what was no longer serving us. By letting go, we created space to let in the infinite possibilities that are available to us. Then we began to uncover what has been holding us back and discovered that we have the power to (re)write our stories by changing the script in our self-talk.

Our next step is to dive deep to create a vision by leaning into desire and intention.

In this chapter, we will:

- Use your desires to create a vision for the future
- Learn to set intentions that count
- Discover how to begin living today in a way that feels effortlessly authentic to you

As we move towards your vision, you will begin to feel a noticeable shift happening from within. This shift occurs when we move out of powerlessness and start to change our lives and harness our power.

DEEPEST DESIRES & INTENTIONS

For thousands of years, philosophers have argued nearly every point of human existence. However, there is only one point on which you can find unanimous agreement across time, generations, and cultures:

"You are what you think about."

When you first decide that you are ready for change, the biggest obstacle you face happens within as you try to quiet all the noise in your head and become reacquainted with your own voice. It can be very hard to get into the driver's seat and to figure our which of your beliefs were impressed on you by others and which are truly your own. Once you are able to quiet down the negative noise swirling around in your head, you are able to turn up the volume on your deepest desires and intentions.

A few years ago, I was invited to speak about personal development for a women's empowerment event. During my speech, I talked about escaping fear and learning to own your power. I asked the audience to close their eyes and picture what their lives would look like if they turned down the negative noise and started listening to the desires that had been whispering within them.

Later in the day, a woman approached me, introducing herself as Avery. I'll never forget what she said to me: "Thank you for helping me to remember all of the things I've wanted for my life that I somehow forgot."

It's true: when we are busy and find ourselves filling our days to the brim answering e-mails and putting out fires, we don't make much time to look within. No wonder it's difficult to figure out our next steps and begin to play bigger in our lives. When we feel held back by everything and everyone that needs our attention, it is hard to make time for ourselves—but it is crucially important to do so.

When we take the time to ask ourselves the questions we need to grow and then listen to the answers, we are able to truly own our power and begin making ourselves a priority.

In writing this book, I designed this chapter to help you to paint a picture of your vision that will ultimately inform your ideal lifestyle. In order to grow, we must ask ourselves the questions that will tell us who we are and what we want in this life. The answers to those questions will powerfully inform how we shape our visions and our future.

Be prepared to get naked and strip down to the bare and honest truth about who you are and what you want your ideal lifestyle to look like. It's going to be big, but it's going to feel oh-so-good—the kind of good that kicks your previous hang-ups to the door, begins to align you with the flow of your life's purpose, and then brings to you the life that you were born to live.

PLANTING SEEDS OF INTENTION

Intentions are the seeds we plant. In his book, *The Strangest Secret*, Earl Nightingale compares the human mind to a farmer's land. He writes, "He may plant in that land whatever he chooses. The land doesn't care what is planted. It's up to the farmer to make the decision."

The same is true of the human mind. **Our mind doesn't care what we plant in it.** Positive or negative, happiness or frustration, gratitude or disgust; it will all grow like seeds planted in fertile soil, and your mind will return to you the harvest of intentions planted. Planting poison ivy or negative thoughts will beget more, just as planting delicious fruits or positive thoughts will allow you to reap the same in land or in your mind.

Think about it this way: if you were to start a new clothing line, the intentions you set would determine the long-term success of your business. For example, what would happen if you desired to create your own clothing line but kept thinking, "There are so many other brands out there, why would anyone want to buy from me? My line is new and not as good as the others."

With this line of thinking, it is likely that your seeds of doubt and your lack of confidence would weave themselves into your marketing, your conversations with investors, and even how your clients perceive themselves in your designs.

On the other hand, if you used your power to shift your thinking to, "I am so excited to share my fresh and innovative clothing designs," your passion will shine through in everything you do. Therefore, your positive intentions reap positive rewards for both your confidence and your bank account.

This is a heavy realization—so what do we do about it? The good news is that **we are in the driver's seat of our own destiny. We reap what we sow.** Since you have control over what you do with your mind, you have the opportunity to paint a picture of your ideal lifestyle.

HOW IT WORKS

Since our goal is to achieve clarity about the lives we want to lead, let's take this opportunity to plant the seeds that will develop into a fertile garden.

We plant seeds of intention by asking ourselves, "What do I want my ideal lifestyle to look like?" By answering this question, you will illuminate the canvas of your mind with the colors of your hopes, dreams, and desires.

It's time to plant your own seeds. Perhaps this is the first time you've considered your future vision, or maybe some of these questions have already come up for you along your journey. Start to picture your ideal day, from the time you wake up in the morning to how you spend your time. Allow yourself to be open and present to what comes up for you as you answer the reflection questions.

OWN YOUR POWER: REFLECTION

How would you like to ...
Eat? Go to bed? Talk to people? Relate to money? Ground or uplift yourself? Work? Talk to yourself?

_____

_____

_____

_____

_____

_____

What would you like to ...
Pay more attention to? Learn? Change in Your Life?

_____

_____

_____

_____

_____

_____

_____

If you had no limitations, where would you ...
Work? Spend your weekends? Go on vacation?

_____

_____

_____

_____

_____

_____

_____

Who would you ...
Spend more time with? Spend less time with? Treat differently?

_____

_____

_____

_____

_____

_____

_____

Intentions are essential to setting the stage for what you want your life to look like. Even more than that, planting seeds of intention can be incredibly powerful in guiding how we want to live and experience our lives. The intention of our vision allows us to use our power to create room for growth, change, and transformation. By connecting to your vision, you are able to define what living life on your own terms truly means to you.

CREATE YOUR THEME

When it comes to our vision, we've talked about our deepest desires and planting the seeds of intention. The third important element to our vision is the development of a theme. In this context, a theme is a word or phrase that resonates with many of your visions, goals, and achievements. It is a way to keep all that you want to work towards in mind.

I learned about the concept of themes from transformational strategist Martine Holston. At first, I resisted creating a theme. I didn't want another thing on my "to-do" list—I was already drinking the green juice, going to yoga, reading books, and getting enough sleep. Adding the creation of a "theme" to the mix immediately felt daunting. However, the most interesting thing I've since learned about themes is that they aren't at all about having another thing to do; rather, they represent a different way of being.

Themes are all about thinking forward, keeping your eye on the prize, and knowing where you are headed. Themes are important because they allow us to reflect on what has worked for us in the past. Reflection provides the space we need to evolve and become the best versions of ourselves.

HOW IT WORKS

We've busted through limiting beliefs, decided what our purpose is along the road ahead, and we've planted seeds of intention. Now, here is your chance to give forward momentum to your vision ahead. Think back to the intention-creating goddess you defined in the previous questions. Then, use this reflection to put together a vision that will be a true impression of how you want to experience your life. Planting the seeds of intention and vision will help you to bring past and future together to reflect and move forward.

OWN YOUR POWER: REFLECTION

Consider the past 365 days and ask yourself: What are the memories that you want to celebrate? What are the moments you want to let go of?

Your three biggest wins in the past year:

1. _____
2. _____
3. _____

The three biggest "obstacles" you want to leave behind:

1. _____
2. _____
3. _____

Now, let's go a little deeper.

Who do you want to be in the next 365 days?

_____

_____

_____

_____

_____

_____

_____

What do you desire to feel, do, and have in the next year?

_____

_____

_____

_____

_____

_____

_____

If you were to write a journal entry looking back one year from today, how would you complete this sentence? *"I am so happy and grateful now that ..."*

_____

_____

_____

_____

_____

_____

_____

From your reflection, list a few potential theme words that resonate with you:

_____

_____

_____

_____

What one theme word represents how you want to show up and shine in the year ahead? _____

HOW CHRISTINE, MEGHAN, JILL, AND JESSICA CREATED THEIR VISIONS

I lost my momentum and needed a serious kick in the butt to get me going. Having clear follow-up directions after each call gave me the accountability I was missing. Bailey got me to take action in the nicest way possible. I loved the lifestyle design exercise where we went deeper into the different aspects of my overall vision. I got clear on where I wanted my life, relationships, and business to be spiritually, mentally, financially, physically, and emotionally!

– **Christine Haz**, *Inspired Event Planner & Founder of GalasandGrace.com*

Before working with Bailey, I only had a small vision of what I wanted. Bailey helped me figure out exactly what I wanted my business to look & feel like, and to design the mission I had for myself and my clients. Without Bailey's help, I would still only be dreaming of having my own coaching business. She is so good and passionate at what she does … I would recommend her services to anyone looking to get the life they've dreamed of! Thanks, Bailey!

– **Meghan Cleveland**, *Holistic Health Coach at MeghanCleveland.com*

Since coaching with Bailey, I have truly begun to understand myself and how to achieve what is most important to me. My fears seem to easily melt away as I can now focus on what is truly delicious to me in my everyday life. Answers for simple everyday tasks to major life decisions come with a certain clarity which allows me to build a roadmap for my life with confidence. I don't always know where I'm going to end up in life, but working with Bailey has given me the direction I've always craved. I look forward to my future now instead of being scared of what's ahead.

– **Jill Spinnenweber,** *Maryland*

Bailey served as a coach to me in utilizing individual strengths and gifts to foster personal development in others. Through her guidance and mentorship, my dreams are now realities.

– **Jessica Ford,** *Fitness Focus Collection*

"People are always blaming their circumstances for what they are. I don't believe in circumstances. The people who get on in this world are the people who get up and look for the circumstances they want, and if they can't find them, make them."

~ GEORGE BERNARD SHAW

CHAPTER SIX

Action

We are wired to take action. As ambitious women, action tends to be our default setting. When we want something, we are ready to make it happen. But as I cautioned you earlier in this book, taking action before figuring out what stands in your way will only keep you more blocked.

When we take time to figure out what has held us back in the past and to get clear about where we want to go in the future, not only are our actions longer-lasting, but they are also more powerful.

In this chapter, we will:

- Frame your vision from Chapter Five in terms of concrete goals
- Learn to set intentions that count
- Discover how to begin living today in a way that feels authentic to you

On this journey together, we first explored our limiting beliefs. Then, we examined our self-talk. Next, we listened within to discover our vision and desires. Now, you will put all of your hard work into motion by taking action to own your power.

TAKING ACTION

Have you ever wondered why a person who becomes successful tends to continue to become even more successful? Similarly, it seems that someone who has failed once often continues to fail.

As Earl Nightingale shares in his recording, *The Strangest Secret*, "The difference is goals. **People with goals succeed because they know where they're going.** Failures, on the other hand, believe that their lives are shaped by circumstances. They believe that things happen to them rather than believing that they can make things happen."

When it comes to owning our power, the only limits come from within.

In this chapter, we will examine how we can get into the driver's seat and achieve our goals. We will step out of our perceived circumstances and begin to identify where we can start taking action today.

Goals with soul stick. When we take the time to plant seeds of intention, they have far more sticking power than sweeping declarations such as, "This will be the year I lose twenty pounds!" or "I'm finally going to quit my job!" The truth is that in order to make anything happen, you've got to have a vision about what you want and an informed action plan on how you will accomplish your goals. This chapter will help you to create an action plan to own your power.

Goals help to keep us on the road to our destiny. Goals provide mile markers along the roadmap of our life. Because we have the control to decide where we want to go, we have the opportunity to take ourselves anywhere.

Take this moment to ask yourself:

"Where do I want to go?"

It doesn't matter as much where your mother thinks you should be headed, or what your partner or even your best friend thinks is the best destination for you. **What matters the most is knowing where you want to go.** Without having a vision, we have no direction.

I've been there—feeling foggy and unsure of my next steps, I didn't believe that I had a vision. I didn't feel pulled in any particular direction. However, when I took the first few steps outlined in this book, I found that I was able to turn up the volume on my vision and desire. When I pulled back the layers of what wasn't working for me, what had previously been holding me back, all of a sudden I started to hear a voice. At first, the voice seemed unrecognizable, but after I sat with it for a while, I found that this voice was my power—and that, the more I listened to it, the louder it became.

During the most difficult part of my journey—the time that I was experiencing adrenal fatigue—I attended a vision board workshop. While everyone around me seemed to have a clear idea of what to do, I had no clue where to start. I began by simply flipping through magazines, tearing out any page that spoke to me. After I'd gone through six or seven, I took the torn-out pages and examined them again. I began to see patterns: images of happy couples of all ages; images of children and families;

beautiful vacation destinations. I began cutting and pasting to my board.

I'll admit that even after completing the vision board, I wasn't sure of what each image meant to me. But once I'd cleared away more layers of resistance and fear, my vision became clearer—and once my vision was clear, I was able to set goals for myself, my relationship, and my career. I was able to move towards everything I desired.

You've already gotten clear about your vision; the next step is setting goals that align with your vision.

Let's consider the four most significant areas of our lives:

- Self
- Health
- Relationships
- Career

In the reflection on the next page, we will focus on these four distinct areas to further define how you would like life to look. We will start with Self and Health and then move onto Relationships and Career. The reason that we start with Self and Health first is because, without vision in these areas in our life, we are unable to be present or give fully in our relationships and work.

Look at each of these goal areas and write a simple sentence that depicts where you would like to be six months from now. For example, a potential Health goal might be, "Sleep seven to eight hours each night, and wake up feeling well-rested."

OWN YOUR POWER: REFLECTION

What Are Your Goals?

SELF	HEALTH
Life is all about *you*. Just as your purpose is what you say it is, your life goals are exactly what you say they are.	Without health, we have a bleak future. We need our health to provide the life force to carry out our goals and ambitions.
CAREER/WORK	**RELATIONSHIPS**
Let's think of work in this sense as what you would do all day, every day if money wasn't a concern.	It's been said that you are the sum of the five people you spend the most time with. Who are these people, and how would you like your time together to be spent?

TIME TO TAKE ACTION

This is where the rubber meets the road. Your action steps are where your true destiny comes alive. In fact, your action steps act as a compass for the directions you must follow on the road to success. As we have learned in this chapter, the difference between people who succeed and people who fail is their belief in the locus of control. We succeed when we believe we have the power to make things happen rather than simply feeling like things happen to us. As Tony Robbins says, "The path to success is to take massive, determined action."

Reflect back again on the foundation we've created in the previous chapters of this book. Each chapter along the journey has prepared you to create the action steps that will allow you to live the life you're destined to live. Remember, this book has been designed to help you in busting through limiting beliefs and re-writing your story along the road ahead.

Once again, as we learned from the quote from Ralph Waldo Emerson, when it comes to our belief system, **we are what we think about all day long.**

It's my job to give you the tools—but only you can decide to take those tools out and use them. You are ready to take action when you believe that you are powerful and can make things happen—when you no longer feel like the victim of your life, void of power.

Are you ready to take massive action to own your power and create the life you want?

In the Reflection on the previous page, you determined your goals and destinations. Now we want to make them stick.

We are able to achieve our goals when we can attach emotion to our stated desires. It's not enough to say we want something or even to be able to visualize ourselves attaining our goal. **What makes us follow through and accomplish our goals quickly and with lasting success is to know how accomplishing a goal will make us *feel*.** When you think about accomplishing the goals in the previous reflection, how do you feel?

HOW IT WORKS

In the next reflection, take time to write how you will feel once you have reached your goal. Use your ability to not only picture your future accomplishments but to connect to your body as you envision your desires. How does it feel?

OWN YOUR POWER: REFLECTION
How Do You Feel Living Your Goal?

SELF	HEALTH
CAREER/WORK	RELATIONSHIPS

By deciding how we want to feel, we ensure that the journey we take to reach our destination is just as sweet and enjoyable as the destination itself.

In addition to attaching feeling to your goals, you must also attach your beliefs to them. Whether or not you *believe* you can accomplish your goals determines your success at creating a life that you love. If you still have any doubt about your own capability, keep in mind what we learned in Chapter Two: understanding your belief systems is essential in identifying roadblocks. If your belief system supports you, owning your power means that you are able to predict your own success even before you've taken action.

ACTION PLANNER

When it comes to taking action, planning ahead will always help us to stay in alignment with our vision. Taking action can be a slippery slope if not infused with intention. Here's why: driven women tend to over-fill our plates. We tend to take on too much, then shut down once we are overwhelmed. This ultimately keeps us from reaching our desired destination.

By planning your actions in alignment with your vision and intentions, your actions become much more powerful than when you are simply crossing things off your to-do list.

We are going to take action a little differently than we may have in the past. Instead of having a running to-do list, I want you to consider: what are the accomplishments that would support you in feeling the way that you desire?

For example, if you desire to feel *present* and *connected* in your relationships, perhaps weekly date nights with friends or monthly farmers' market visits with the family will be the "make-it-happen" action that will support you in achieving your goal.

HOW IT WORKS

For each of the most impactful lifestyle areas—Self, Health, Relationships, and Career—determine your intention. What is the biggest result that you desire to achieve? Next, what are the three (just three!) most impactful "make-it-happen" actions that you must take in support of your intention? Finally, you will work on creating clear action steps that will take you where you need to be to achieve your desired accomplishments or experiences.

OWN YOUR POWER ACTION GUIDE

SELF

Intention: _____

_____

_____

_____

Make-It-Happen Actions:

1. _____
2. _____
3. _____

HEALTH

Intention: _____

_____

_____

_____

Make-It-Happen Actions:

1. _____
2. _____
3. _____

CAREER/WORK

Intention: _____

_____

_____

_____

Make-It-Happen Actions:

1. _____
2. _____
3. _____

RELATIONSHIPS

Intention: _____

_____

_____

_____

Make-It-Happen Actions:

1. _____
2. _____
3. _____

Part of owning your power is living your life with intention. We feel out of control and disempowered when our lives feel like they are unfolding haphazardly. The interesting thing about the desire for freedom is that the more structure we integrate into our lives, the more success and freedom we actually experience. Living an intentional life means having the structure to enjoy the journey rather than feeling as if we are simply putting out one fire after another.

Committing to your make-it-happen actions means committing to yourself. It means choosing you. And ultimately, it means that you have decided that your dreams and desires are the most important thing in designing a life you love and a life that you lovingly share with others.

CAT'S JOURNEY

Before working with Bailey, I was struggling with keeping myself clear and focused on the actions that would drive and grow my business.

Since working with Bailey, I've done a complete 180-degree turnaround! Bailey has helped me hone in on the activities that will best suit me in the short term, supporting my long-term objectives. I know I can come to her with anything - I mean anything - and she can help me sift through it and pull out the truth that will help keep me motivated and focused on achieving my goals.

I can say with all honesty and sincerity that I would not be where I am, or on the path to where I want to be, without Bailey's help and guidance.

I'm excited to start generating the revenue that I thought would never happen for me, giving me the gift of financial freedom and flexibility in my life. For me, part of that includes getting out there in a bigger way (e.g., speaking), and Bailey is the perfect role model for that!

- **Cat Stancik**, *Strategist at Catalytic Change, LLC*

CHRISTINE TOOK ACTION

Working with Bailey has been the best gift I have ever given myself! Before we started our work together, I was stuck, depressed, and desperately trying to discover my purpose and path. Then Bailey came into my life, and this magical world of possibilities opened up for me. Bailey has this amazing gift of listening to my thoughts, then helping me tune into their real messages and clearly respond with true intention.

While working with Bailey, I have found this amazing strength in myself to boldly honor the person I am, to create freedom in my lifestyle to dream big and play without restriction, and the ability to channel my chaotic thoughts into easy steps and achievable goals. There is so much I have to say and not enough room to write about just how profoundly working with Bailey has helped me live a life I didn't even know was possible.

- **Christine Haskin**, *Chicago*

"It takes courage to endure the sharp pains of self-discovery, rather than choose the dull pain of unconsciousness that would last the rest of our lives."

~ MARIANNE WILLIAMSON

CHAPTER SEVEN

Power

If we want our lives to look differently, we've got to do things in a different way. Owning your power doesn't happen when you judge yourself for "not getting it right." Instead, it happens when you've decided to do things differently in order to live a more vibrant life.

There's an interesting paradox that exists as we create new pathways and belief systems. **As we start to make a shift away from our old beliefs and ways of doing things, we sometimes become afraid of confidently stepping into our power.**

I've seen this happen to myself as well as many other women on the path to living their best life. Fear of success emerges as we transition from an old way of thinking into a new way of being.

The fear of success arises when we are at the precipice of owning our power; it comes to the surface as we step into a bigger leadership role or challenge ourselves to do something that we have never done before.

Why are we afraid to succeed?

- We're scared to fail.
- We're scared to try—because we are afraid of rejection.
- We're scared to put ourselves out there.
- We're scared of being judged.

Sometimes we don't take the leap because we're afraid of the unknown. The thought, "What if?" makes us shrink back.

But when we allow our feet to get stuck in cement, we rob ourselves of what could be.

When we are afraid, we might squash chance, risk, or even opportunity. By letting fear take the wheel, we miss the exit onto the road of success. The journey towards growth and our biggest dreams often includes a bumpy road of frustration, failed starts, and a few flat tires. Don't forget that it also includes sunshine.

POWER IN ACTION

I clearly remember navigating this road as I began to play a bigger game in my life. I finally had the chance to deliver a keynote speech, something I had long dreamt about. However, when the opportunity arrived, so did my fears, anxieties, and perceived inadequacies.

On a crisp, sunny day in the fall of 2012, I drove to the auditorium. I glanced in the rearview mirror: I looked like the picture of confidence. I had a new suit, a fresh blow-out—I had even bought a new pair of shoes for my keynote speech. But beneath my sunglasses, I was feeling anything but confident. I was nervous and worried about rejection.

I'd talked to many groups of people about finding motivation and making change in their lives before, but this time I was frozen in fear. It was my first time as a keynote speaker, my first time in front of a sold-out audience. I believed that if I failed, it would be big.

As I pulled into my parking spot, I thought, "perhaps I will just call and say I got a flat, maybe I can say I'm sick." But I knew that at this moment I had to prove to myself that I could do it.

As I sat in the parking lot, I decided that **now was the time that I had to walk my talk.** I began using each of the tools I have shared in this book. First, I needed to get unstuck. I asked myself—what is my vision? How will doing this speech make a difference in my life? Next, I had to release my fear—what was holding me back? What triggered my resistance? What negative belief related to delivering this keynote?

By understanding what was holding me back, I understood that owning my power meant choosing to save myself. It was time to rewrite my story. I quickly grabbed an old receipt from my glove compartment to jot down a self-talk cycle. I needed to see for myself the belief system shift.

First, I wrote the negative words swirling in my head: *Failure. I can't do it. Too much pressure.*

Then I wrote down the feelings associated with these words: *Fear. Inadequacy.*

Finally, I wrote down the action I was taking: *Sitting frozen in fear in my car.*

It was time to change things.

I drew out the same self-talk cycle, but this time, I shifted it to the positive. Almost immediately, a weight lifted from my shoulders. I wrote down the belief *I am capable and prepared.* It made me feel powerful. The action I would take would be to get out of the car and give the speech.

However, I knew that my newfound confidence might only last me until I was standing at the podium—unless I found a mantra to become the new soundtrack in my mind. I wanted to step off that stage feeling like a rock star, so I needed an affirmation that would reflect my confidence and power.

One word emerged, and it felt right: *Truth.*

I could do that. I could share my truth. But to embody my story of truth, I needed to know what that would look like.

As crazy as it sounds, I reclined the seat of my car, closed my eyes, and mentally walked through my next steps. I pictured myself shaking hands with the event hosts, being miked up, hearing the crowd go quiet, listening to myself be introduced, and then finally taking the stage. I pictured myself looking out into the audience and smiling, knowing that I had a story to share and some wisdom from my own journey that might help someone in the audience. I pictured myself growing more confident with each moment on stage and closing with applause.

I realized that I had the capability to own my power and move beyond my fear. Finally, I was able to let go of my fear and take the stage. Once on stage, I shared my truth, my purpose, and my authenticity. I felt like a rock star—and from the standing ovation I received, I believe the audience felt the same.

The road to success, although sometimes rocky, allows us to appreciate the sweetness of progress, the gift of trial and error, and the pride of owning our power.

We are afraid to succeed because we fear the road less traveled.

However, **we are all capable of great things, amazing things — of truly capturing our genius—if we are brave enough to chase after our dreams.** Don't lose hope!

After I convinced myself to open the car door, I knew that the fear I was feeling wasn't real. I was afraid of all the things that "could" go wrong, rather than embracing the possibility of success.

I'm going to let you in on a little secret. When we first try to do big things, great big things, our egos will freak out. This might sound surprising: isn't your ego always pumping you up, keeping you focused on yourself and your needs? While that may be true, your ego likes to maintain a sense of equilibrium. It likes for everything to stay the same, without change, without growth. When we push ourselves to grow, our ego will shout nasty things at us. It will drum up old anxieties, worries, and fears from the past in an effort to deter you from doing that big thing that calls from your soul.

This happens often when we take on leadership roles—when we are ready to step into the bright light of success, to cross over from the old belief systems to the brand-new. It happened to me when I took the stage for my keynote speech. But when I decided to move past my fear and take the stage, I embraced my vulnerability. I felt broken open, and was ready to share my most authentic truth.

Owning your power is about opening up to vulnerability without giving up.

To be successful, you have to put yourself out there and embrace the possibility of simply trying. At times you might stumble, but when you are clear about your intention, vision, and motivation, you'll get back up and try again. Your desire for a new life is so much more important than the old beliefs that no longer serve you.

Vulnerability doesn't mean being a victim; rather, it means letting go of what other people think about you and instead having the courage to authentically be yourself. It also means letting go of your ego and your own self-doubt.

If we don't change, we don't grow. If we don't evolve, we just stay the same. By taking this journey, you've decided to commit yourself to life on your own terms.

The next step towards growth is clearing away the voice of self-doubt.

OWN YOUR POWER: REFLECTION
Who I Am

Consider how you show up in the world, the gifts you have to share with the world, and what it means to truly embrace your authenticity.

How the world sees you

What unique strength/ability allows you to be successful? What unique gift do you share with the world?

_____

_____

_____

_____

_____

_____

When people talk about the impact you've made in their lives, what do you get complimented for the most?

_____

_____

_____

_____

_____

What has shaped your most authentic self

What three life lesson have shaped you the most? What did you learn from them?

Experience #1 _____

_____

_____

Lesson: _____

Experience #2 _____

_____

_____

Lesson: _____

Experience #3 _____

_____

_____

Lesson: _____

Who you really are

What are the top three activities make you feel useful, strong, and live-out-loud alive?

1. _____
2. _____
3. _____

When telling the story of your life, what do you want to be known for?

_____

_____

_____

_____

_____

_____

THE POWER OF VULNERABILITY

As humans, we are designed to perceive vulnerability as weakness. Naturally, we don't want to feel susceptible, weak, or powerless. Instead, we want to feel all-knowing and capable. We want to have all the answers. **But when playing bigger in your life, you're going somewhere you've never been—how can you possibly know what to expect?**

As Brené Brown has shared in her work, vulnerability is not weakness; it's our greatest measure of courage. Fear can keep us paralyzed from truly connecting with our power, keeping us from the joys of vulnerability and authenticity.

When we are vulnerable, we are real. Being authentic is the most important gift we can give ourselves. By confronting our fear, we will push farther ahead on the path to success. Pushing through fear will help us to be better leaders in this world by being open, vulnerable, and human.

You can do it. You can move through fear to become your best self.

Whatever it is you're working on in your life — whether a challenging job, task, project, person, or event—you can live the life you've always imagined. By owning your power, you can and will succeed.

Stumbling through fear is better than freaking out.

When your heart beats faster and your palms get clammy, remember, fear is your compass. It's calling you to rise above small thinking and to play bigger. See it. Feel it. Observe and Catch it. Then, walk straight through it.

After all, if you never step on stage, you'll miss your standing ovation!

LET'S KEEP TALKING ...

Congratulations on finishing *Own Your Power!* Not only did you sense the life-changing content in this book, you acted. You purchased it, read it, finished it. Not that it surprises me—you are that busy person who takes on more, completes the task, hits the goal. You wouldn't have picked up this book otherwise.

And because you're a type-A overachiever—dotting the I's, crossing the T's, and generally going above and beyond in everything you do—I'll bet you completed the reflections in each chapter, too. Great!

(If not – no worries, it's all good! It's never too late. Gently and lovingly, I invite you to go back and fill those in.)

Whether you simply read the book and/or completed the reflections, you may be wondering ...

... Now what?

This book is the beginning of a conversation—a conversation with a part of yourself that you may have quieted until now.

And, as comprehensive as this book is—and although I've shown you step-by-step on how to get to the deep, inner work where true freedom and fulfillment lives—it can only scratch the surface.

That is the nature of this journey, my friend: the further down the tunnel we go, the more we unearth. In fact, in the course of reading this book, you may have uncovered more questions than you started with. You may be feeling inspired, motivated … and a little freaked out.

Hey, I get it! As you may have guessed from the first few chapters of this book: I have *so* been there, done that.

So, what do you do with all these revelations and reflections swirling around in your head?

You take action. It's how you're wired.

First, connect with others on this journey. You are not alone, and it is nearly impossible to do this work on our own. The process goes so much faster (and is so much more fun!) when you're in awesome, like-minded company. **I invite you to continue the conversation with me and the many women in our community by joining our Own Your Power: Inspired Living Lounge community on Facebook, at Facebook. com/ InspiredLivingLounge.** There, we inspire and support one another by sharing our journeys of success and triumph from the obstacles that have held us back in the past.

You can also check out OwnYourPowerBook.com/bonuses for additional free resources and tools to help you own your power.

But wait, there's more!

At OwnYourPowerBook.com, you'll find articles and free

video tutorials on topics vital to your success—from creating rock-solid confidence to tapping your strength to move past fear.

Okay, great. You've got tons of tools to work with. Right now, you have in your hands all the resources, stories, tools, and opportunity you need to make powerful changes in your life. But what are you going to do with them? How can you make all the work you just did stick?

Don't worry: I have created a solution to keep the momentum going, and support you in deeper learning and taking further action!

THE OWN YOUR POWER MASTERY PROGRAM

Are you ready to go deeper, truly implement and incorporate this work into your life, and create lasting, life-changing, powerhouse transformation?

Then join me and get the straight-up, no-woo-woo, real deal on what's holding you back from a life you love, and the step-by-step strategy on how to move past it.

I invite you to get past "stuck" to the live the life you've always wanted – with the community, support, and tools to make it happen—for real, and for good this time.

If you are DONE with ...

Running on the hamster wheel of achievement with no sense of fulfillment ...

Meeting goals with no satisfaction…

Feeling like there has to be something more…

And, if you are ready for real, tangible results …

IT'S TIME.
YOUR TIME.

It's time to take your life where YOU want it to go, instead of being pulled along.

Getting into the driver's seat of your life is a choice. So If you're feeling called, come on over and check it out at

OwnYourPowerMastery.com

You CAN know what you want, and actually get it! It would be my honor to be your partner on this journey, and gently guide you step-by-step to unlock your true potential. **You've got this!**

I look forward to seeing you on the other side!

With love,

Bailey

ACKNOWLEDGMENTS

I am so very grateful for the love, encouragement, and support of so many people who have given me the tools to bring this book to life. There are countless people in my life without whom, if our paths had not crossed, I would not be who I am today—and certainly not able to share the mission of empowerment through coaching that fuels me. For that, I am endlessly thankful.

To Fabienne Fredrickson and the whole Boldheart/Client Attraction team, you have given me the guiding light and missing piece that my passion has needed, thank you for teaching me what it means to authentically share my "brownies."

To my editors, Bryna Haynes and Rebecca van Laer, I am so grateful for your guidance, kindness, and grace.

To my team: you guys have absolutely rocked it, and I couldn't be more thankful to know that you have my back.

To my clients (who have always been my true teachers), for allowing me to accompany them into the darkest places and create the brightest paths for them to own their power and become the best versions of themselves. Our work together has allowed me to write each word in this book with full conviction, knowing the change coaching can create.

To Sarah Jenks and Nisha Moodley, my very first coaching inspirations, thank you for holding space and creating the Live Free Retreat that birthed the next chapter in my journey and guided me to the evolution of my dreams.

To all of my friends, who have been by my side to celebrate and cry. I am most especially thankful to Jessica Gaestel, thank you for thirty years of friendship; here's to (at least) thirty more! To Amy Dube for being my go-to biz wiz and favorite yummy yogi; to Dr. Nicole Rivera for the fierce competition and fierce love. (Hopefully you'll learn to like me someday, ha!) To Dina Cole for being my "big sister," and teaching me the fine art of finesse. And to René Ponticello, for all the reasons that distance and time never really matter.

To all the mentors who have provided guidance and the most loving care—Mary Rower, Jennifer Flynn, and Hal Ornestein, I appreciate your time and wisdom more than you will ever know.

And finally, but most especially, to my family: my husband, Bobby, who has always been my biggest cheerleader, moving heaven and earth to make my dreams come true; and to our daughter, Phoebe, who has taught me the true meaning of balance. To my sisters, Whit and Kait, both of whom share a love for travel, exploring the world, and embracing the cultural experiences that life has to offer: thank you for being two of the smartest chicks I know. To my parents, who have given me so much support and love to expand to my potential: my mother, who taught me the power held within strong women; and my father, who taught me to pave my own way and believe in myself.

And, lastly, to you, the soul who has now picked up *Own Your Power*: may the words in this book give you the power you need to believe in yourself and unlock your true potential.

You've got this!

ABOUT THE AUTHOR

Bailey Frumen

B ailey Frumen, MSW, LCSW, is a psychotherapist, writer, speaker, and transformational success coach helping ambitious women leaders and entrepreneurs to ditch fear and take action on living lives they love.

She has been named one of the "Top 20 Life Coaches to Watch" by PopExpert.com. Bailey's work has been published in *Huffington Post, Elephant Journal, Aspire Magazine, Natural Awakenings,* and numerous guest blogs. She is a featured author in the women's anthology *Inspiration for a Woman's Soul: Opening To Gratitude & Grace* through Inspired Living Publishing.

Through her Own Your Power Mastery Program, live events, speaking engagements, and transformational coaching, Bailey helps women around the world to master their mindset by transcending fear, overwhelm, and uncertainty. With over ten years of experience helping women to live their best lives, she guides women leaders and entrepreneurs to feel more confident by mastering their mindsets and living the lives they've always wanted.

Bailey lives with her husband, daughter, and two pups, and spends her time on the beaches of New Jersey, the Outer Banks of North Carolina, and Rincón, Puerto Rico. She loves yoga, riding bikes, reading books, surfing, and spending time at the beach with her family.

Bailey can usually be found with passport in hand, but you can keep track of her on Instagram & Twitter @BaileyFrumen. Visit **BaileyFrumen.com** to learn more about her work and mission.

Made in the USA
Middletown, DE
25 July 2017